**AUBURN HILLS PUBLIC LIBRARY**
3400 E. Seyburn Drive
AUBURN HILLS, MI 48326

# Driving around the USA
## Automobiles in American Life

# Driving around the USA
## Automobiles in American Life

Martin W. Sandler

OXFORD
UNIVERSITY PRESS

*For Winslow, on the eve of his getting his driver's license.*

## Acknowledgments

The author wishes to thank Karen Fein, Nancy Toff, and the Blackhawk Museum for the help they provided in shaping this book. As always, Carol Sandler has made many contributions. A special acknowledgment is due Nancy Hirsch, whose guidance and editorial skills have been invaluable.

## Picture Credits

Collection of the author: 9, 25, 27; © Bettmann/Corbis: 45; © California Department of Transportation, photographer Duncan McIntosh: 51; © Corbis: 37; Detroit Industry, North Wall, 1932–1993, Diego M. Rivera, Gift of Edsel B. Ford. Photograph © 2001 The Detroit Institute of Arts: 20; © Disney Enterprises: 53; Federal Highway Administration, photographs by Jim Lyle: cover, frontispiece; © Owen Franken/Corbis: 49; Duke University: 16, 35; General Motors: 58; Grand Prix Driving School: 55; Photograph appears courtesy of Inter-Continental Hotels Group: 36; Kansas State Historical Society: 8; Library of Congress: chapter openers, 10, 13, 15, 17, 18, 19, 23, 24, 26, 28, 30, 33; The Mack Trucks Historical Museum: 50; National Historic Route 66 Foundation: 31, Naylor Collection: 7, 38, 41, 43, 46; Photo courtesy http://philip.greenspun.com: 47; University of Virginia Center for Applied Biomechanics: 56

# OXFORD
## UNIVERSITY PRESS

Oxford   New York
Auckland   Bangkok   Buenos Aires   Cape Town   Chennai
Dar es Salaam   Delhi   Hong Kong   Istanbul   Karachi   Kolkata
Kuala Lumpur   Madrid   Melbourne   Mexico City   Mumbai
Nairobi   São Paulo   Shanghai   Taipei   Tokyo   Toronto

Copyright © 2003 by Martin W. Sandler

Design by Alexis Siroc

Published by Oxford University Press, Inc.
198 Madison Avenue, New York, New York, 10016
www.oup-usa.org

Oxford is a registered trademark of Oxford University Press

All rights reserved. No part of this publication may be reproduced, stored in a retrieval system, or transmitted, in any form or by any means, electronic, mechanical, photocopying, recording, or otherwise, without the prior permission of Oxford University Press.

Library of Congress Cataloging-in-Publication Data

Sandler, Martin W.
  Driving around the USA : automobiles in American life / Martin W. Sandler.
      p. cm. — (Transportation in American life)
  Includes bibliographical references and index.
  ISBN 0-19-513230-0
  1. Transportation, Automotive—United States. 2. Transportation, Automotive—Social aspects—United States. 3. Automobiles—Social aspects—United States.
  I. Title. II. Series.
  HE5623 .S247 2003
  388.3'0973—dc21                                          2003000987

Printing number:   9   8   7   6   5   4   3   2   1

Printed in Hong Kong on acid-free paper

ON THE COVER: **As imagined in a 1935 painting, viaducts, or raised roads, helped improve safety and reduce traffic delays.**

FRONTISPIECE: **Motorists celebrate the opening of a one-mile stretch of paved road in rural Michigan on July 4th, 1909.**

# Contents

**CHAPTER 1**
The Birth of the Automobile  6

**CHAPTER 2**
America on Wheels  14

**CHAPTER 3**
Automania  22

**CHAPTER 4**
The Indispensable Auto  32

**CHAPTER 5**
Classic Cars, Dream Machines, Hot Rods, and Lowriders  40

**CHAPTER 6**
The Car Culture  48

Timeline  59
Places to Visit  60
Further Reading  61
Index  62

# CHAPTER 1
# The Birth of the Automobile

*"You'll have to teach yourself to drive it; nobody in town can show you how. Nobody has seen a horseless carriage, let alone driven one. But luckily an instruction book has come with the machine."*

—*Kearney* (Nebraska) *Times,* 1894

In 1876 the United States marked its 100th birthday. There was much to celebrate. The nation was recovering from the wounds of the Civil War, which had torn it apart little more than a decade earlier. Pioneers were settling the vast American West and turning it into one of the most productive farming areas in the world. At the same time, immigrants from around the globe were pouring into America, making it the symbol of hope and opportunity for people everywhere. And thanks to a remarkable nationwide spirit of invention, Americans were able to travel around the nation faster and more conveniently than their grandparents had ever thought would be possible.

Railroad tracks linked the continent from coast to coast. Steamboats and sailing vessels carried passengers up and down rivers and across lakes and sounds. Horse-drawn trolleys provided city dwellers with the best system of urban transit yet developed. And in 1888 electric trolleys would begin to make travel within the city even more efficient.

Yet many people were still not satisfied. They dreamed of a vehicle that would not be tied to the rails, as were the trains and the trolleys. They wanted something they could drive themselves, something that could go anywhere any time they wanted. Although no one had given such a vehicle a name, what they yearned for was the automobile.

The automobile was born in Europe in the late 1700s. This was made possible by the invention of the steam engine, and then of a way to use the steam supplied by the engine to turn the wheels of a car. A French army engineer named Nicolas Joseph Cugnot is credited with being the first man to drive a self-propelled road vehicle. In 1769 he built a tractor-like machine, powered by a huge copper steam engine that hung out beyond the front wheel. This cumbersome contraption traveled fewer than five miles per hour, and

This steam tricycle, which traveled through the streets of Washington D.C. in 1888, was a forerunner of the steam-powered automobile.

it was so difficult to maneuver that when Cugnot took it out on the streets of Paris and attempted to negotiate a curve, he banged into a wall and the vehicle turned over. The police, alarmed at the sight of the vehicle, put Cugnot in jail and confiscated his invention. Though Cugnot never again drove his machine on a public street, he had proved that a self-propelled road vehicle was possible.

Cugnot's accomplishment inspired other European inventors. Between 1801 and 1803, Englishman Richard Trevithick built and demonstrated four-wheeled, steam-driven vehicles that were able to carry passengers. Observing one of Trevithick's trial runs, in which his machine carried eight people up a half-mile-long hill, an eyewitness marveled at the fact that the vehicle traveled "faster than a man could walk."

The electric car was the first automobile capable of traveling a mile a minute, but it was the social status the vehicle gave its owners that, to many, was its greatest asset.

Driving around the USA

The inventor Oliver Evans could rightly claim to be the father of the self-propelled road vehicle in America. In 1805 he built an enormous, steam-driven river dredge that was to be used to improve Philadelphia's harbor. In order to drive the machine through the city's streets to the harbor, he mounted it on wheels. He had another purpose in mind as well. As Cugnot and Trevithick had demonstrated in Europe, Evans wanted to show Americans that what he called a "steam-wagon" could be a practical means of transportation.

In the years following Evans's demonstration, many American inventors experimented with steam cars. But it was not until the late 1860s that they worked out the kinks and made stream-driven road vehicles a reality. Once this was accomplished, pioneer automakers went at their task with a passion.

In the late 1800s, more than 100 manufacturers were involved in building what were called steamers. Of these men, the most successful were the identical twin brothers Francis E. and Freelan O. Stanley. The Stanleys were born in Kingfield, Maine. They made both a name

A Stanley Steamer climbs a hill on the way to a first-place finish in an early auto race. The Stanley brothers were racing enthusiasts and used the sport to advertise the capabilities of their cars.

for themselves and a considerable fortune through a photographic company they owned and operated. But the possibilities of the steam-driven car fascinated them. In 1896 the Stanleys sold their photographic company, opened a factory in Newton, Massachusetts, and began producing steam buggies. In 1899 they built and sold almost 200 Stanley Steamers.

The Stanleys' cars and the steamers built by other manufacturers launched America into the age of the automobile. But there were drawbacks to these pioneer vehicles. The procedure for getting the fire in a steamer's boiler to heat up sufficiently was complicated and time-consuming. Because the steam engine had to be small enough to be practical for use in a car, it was under extremely high pressure. Although there is no record of any steamer

These happy travelers enjoy a ride in their gasoline-powered car. Reporting on the advantages of the internal combustion engine in 1905, *Scientific American* proclaimed that "the age of steam is ended."

Driving around the USA

ever having exploded, the possibility was frightening. This made many who would have loved to own their own car reluctant to purchase one.

By the 1890s, however, battery-powered electric trolleys were fast becoming the rage of American cities. They inspired inventors to develop a new type of self-propelled vehicle designed to combat the drawbacks of the steamers. In 1891 William Morrison, a resident of Des Moines, Iowa, built America's first successful electric car. Morrison's vehicle, which was powered by batteries under the seats, could accommodate six passengers. Soon other manufacturers, including American Electric, Baker, and Columbia, were building electric cars, which quickly became popular. And in many places electric cars caused a sensation. "Ever since [the electric car's] arrival," reported *Western Electrician* magazine in 1892

> the sight of a well-loaded carriage moving along the streets at a spanking pace with no horses in front and apparently with nothing on board to give it motion, was a sight that has been too much even for the wide-awake Chicagoan.... So great has been the curiosity that the owner when passing through the business section has had to appeal to the police to aid him in clearing the way.

With the introduction of the electric car, a significant number of women, particularly wealthy society ladies, took to the driver's seat. The electric cars were noiseless and free of offensive odor. The driver turned the car on with a simple flip of a switch. For many wealthy women, the electric car became a "must" for shopping, taking a spin, and most important, keeping up with their neighbors. Several electric car manufacturers advertised their products with the slogan "The only car for a lady."

The electric vehicles had many advantages over steamers. They were much easier to control, gave off no smoke or fumes, and operated quietly. But these cars had their own particular drawbacks. They could not attain a speed of more than 20 miles per hour and could travel only between 40 and 60 miles before their batteries had to be recharged. Automobile engineers attempting to build pollution-free, more economical electric cars today still struggle to overcome some of these same problems.

Although both steam and electric power had their shortcomings, they enabled the first motorists to take to the road and imagine the extraordinary possibilities of the automobile. But another power source was needed to make these possibilities a reality. As early as the 1860s, various European inventors had been working on internal combustion, or gasoline, engines.

Some 20 years later, two German inventors, Gottlieb Daimler and Karl Benz, working independently of each other, finally succeeded in building the first successful gasoline-powered cars. From that time on, the powerful, durable gasoline engine became the power source for almost all cars, including most of those that people drive today.

The first American to successfully design a gasoline-powered car was a patent attorney and amateur inventor named George B. Selden. But even though he applied for a patent some 10 years before Daimler built his first engine, Selden never took his design beyond the planning stage. The honor of actually producing the first successful gasoline-powered automobile in the United States went to Charles and Frank Duryea. In September 1893 the Duryea brothers drove their experimental car through the streets of Springfield, Massachusetts. There were still many improvements to be made, but as the 19th century drew to an end, the automobile had arrived in America and was here to stay.

In this 1899 cartoon a horse weeps as it is driven in a car to its new home in a museum. By the late 1890s it was clear that the automobile would eventually replace the horse as the main mode of transportation.

The Birth of the Automobile    13

## CHAPTER 2
# America on Wheels

*"The automobile never bites or kicks, never tires on long runs and never sweats in hot weather. It does not require care in the stable and eats only when on the road."*

—Pioneer automaker Ransom Olds, predicting how the automobile would replace the horse as America's favorite form of personal transportation, in the *Chicago Tribune*, 1898

The Duryea brothers' vehicle was the first of millions of gasoline-powered automobiles that would come to fill the country roads and city streets of America. Soon after the brothers' success, other car manufacturers began introducing their own models.

The earliest of these cars, however, were still too costly for the average citizen. Moreover, they presented real problems both for their owners and for the pubic in general. The tires on the early gasoline-driven cars were solid rubber, which made for a very rough ride. The introduction of air-filled tires in the early 1900s made the ride more comfortable, but presented a new problem. The still unperfected air-filled tires were flimsy and could be driven on for only 10 or 12 miles before they were punctured.

Every early gasoline-powered car kicked up a cloud of dust around it, often choking driver and passengers alike. In 1886, Samuel Crawford, a Merna, Nebraska, doctor spoke for many of his colleagues when he warned against "the many dangers of the open road, poisonous fumes, currents of cold air, or in the summertime, choking dust and swarms of small winged insects." And in a nation still dominated by travel by horse, there were other warnings and concerns. "Perhaps the time will come," stated a Texas senator, "when horses will be educated to the point where they will not be afraid of automobiles; but I doubt that, for I have not seen the time yet when I was not afraid of them."

In 1900, a full seven years after the Duryeas' demonstration, only 400 of almost 2,400 automobiles in New York City, Boston, and Chicago were gasoline powered. By the end of the first decade of the 1900s, however, manufacturers of gasoline-driven cars would find ways of making their cars more efficient. Equally important, they would adopt innovative methods of producing them cheaply.

In 1900 almost every automobile company, whether it was constructing cars powered by electricity

In 1918, Henry Ford posed proudly in the first car made by his company. Ford would soon introduce the Model T, which made automobiles affordable to average Americans.

This 1913 song points out the fact that in the early days of the automobile every car owner had to be his own mechanic.

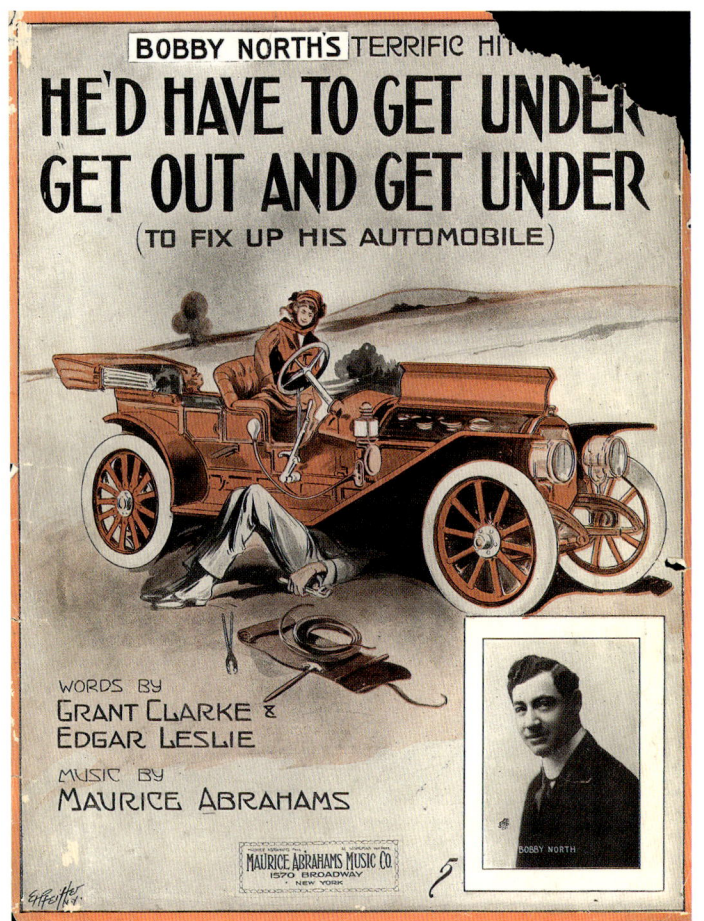

or gasoline, built them in the same manner. Three or four workers gathered around the car's frame and then added parts that were hauled from other areas of the factory. This time-consuming and costly process was the main reason an average automobile cost more than $1,000, which at that time was more than twice what the average American earned in a year. Mass production, however, soon reduced that price to an affordable level.

Pioneer automobile manufacturer Ransom E. Olds was the first person to use a form of mass production to make cars. As early as 1892, Olds saw that the automobile would one day replace the horse as America's favorite form of personal transportation. The auto, he said, "never bites or kicks, never tires on long runs, and never sweats in hot weather. It does not require care in the stable and only eats while on the road."

In 1899 Olds founded the Olds Motor Works in Detroit, Michigan. The first car he built sold for $1,250, and was too expensive to be successful. But Olds was determined to find a way to produce cars that people could afford. He came up with the idea of assembling his automobiles on wheeled platforms. The platforms were rolled to workmen who added specific parts until each automobile was fully

Picnickers dressed for a day in the country enjoy a meal in a secluded spot they had reached in their automobile.

assembled. It was a huge step forward, but it was still not efficient enough to enable Olds to sell his automobiles at a reasonable price. Henry Ford was the man who made that happen.

Ford did not invent the automobile. He did not drive the first car. He did not invent the gasoline engine. But he did something perhaps even more important. He built the most popular automobile Americans have ever known and assembled it in such a way that millions of people could afford to own one. It was Henry Ford who put America on wheels.

Ford grew up near Dearborn, Michigan, a community near Detroit. He was not a particularly good student, but even as a youngster he displayed an unusual talent for working with machinery. Like Ransom Olds, he was also a visionary, a man who understood more than most about how the automobile, once it could be made affordable, would revolutionize the way people moved about.

Perhaps more than any other early carmaker, Ford had a clear idea of what kind of automobile would make that happen. "I will build a motor car for the great multitude," Ford wrote in his 1922 autobiography,

The gigantic workforce at this Buick automobile factory poses proudly in 1913 in front of a banner celebrating their ability to manufacture 40,000 cars a year.

it will be large enough for the family but small enough for the individual to run and care for. It will be constructed of the best materials, by the best men to be hired after the simplest designs that modern engineering can devise. But it will be so low in price that no man making a good salary will be unable to own one—and enjoy with his family the blessings of hours of pleasure in God's great open spaces.

Henry Ford kept his word. After experimenting with several different models, he came up with the Model T (the name has no real meaning). The public would soon affectionately refer to it as the Tin Lizzie.

The Model T, designed to be as uncomplicated as possible, had a strong, durable body and was mounted high to allow it to travel over bumpy roads. The car had two speeds forward and one in reverse. A driver operated it by simply pressing or releasing foot pedals. Unlike most earlier cars, the Tin Lizzie sported a huge top, which protected the driver and passengers from the elements.

Perhaps the key feature of the Model T was that at a time when there were almost no automotive

The Oldsmobile Company was the first to use the slogan "King of the Road" to describe its cars. It was later adopted by several other automobile manufacturers.

20 Driving around the USA

mechanic shops, owners could make any needed repairs themselves. Ford company officials boasted that the entire automobile could be kept going with wire, pliers, and a screwdriver. Not long after it was first built, parts for the car could be purchased in a five-and-ten-cents store.

The Model T fulfilled Henry Ford's goal of producing a car that anyone could drive and maintain. And he made his cars affordable by improving the mass-production techniques that had already been used by Ransom Olds and others. Through trial and error, he finally hit upon a system by which a fast-moving conveyor belt carried all the various parts of a Model T to workers stationed along that belt. "The step forward in assembly," Ford explained in his autobiography, "came when we began taking the work to the men instead of the men to the work."

The largest factory in America at the time, Ford's River Rouge plant was the inspiration for Mexican artist Diego Rivera's mural *Detroit Industry*. Today River Rouge still produces a car every few seconds.

After establishing his assembly line, Ford continued to make improvements designed to lessen the time it took to put his automobiles together. In 1913 it took 12.5 hours to assemble each Model T. The following year, the time had been reduced to 93 minutes. By the mid-1920s, Ford had made so many improvements, both in the mechanical aspects of the assembly line and in the ways in which his workers installed the parts, that his company was turning out a fully assembled Model T every 40 seconds.

By 1925 the Ford factory was producing more than 2 million cars a year at a rate of more than 9,000 a day. More than half the cars in the world were Model T Fords. Most important, this extraordinary production enabled Ford to keep reducing the price of his cars. In 1908, when the Model T was introduced, it sold for $850. By 1916 the price had dropped to $350. In 1925 a spanking new Model T could be purchased for only $240. More than anyone else, Henry Ford made it possible for average Americans to buy their own automobiles.

CHAPTER 3

# Automania

*"The paramount ambition of the average man a few years ago was to own a home and have a bank account. The ambition of the same man today is to own a car...."*

—Moline, Illinois, banker Wallace Ames, 1925

By the end of the first decade of the 1900s, Americans took to the road in a fashion best described as "automania." They clogged city streets and the nation's roads, most of which were narrow and not adequately paved. Some people drove the luxurious Ford models, such as the Model R and the Model S, that Ford eventually produced. They also drove cars made by competing companies, such as General Motors, Chrysler, Packard, Winton, and others. By the late 1920s, there was close to one automobile on the road in the United States for every five Americans.

Once the gasoline engine appeared, the days of the electric cars were numbered. Increasingly, motorists turned to the more powerful, speedier, gasoline-powered vehicles. But the gas-driven automobiles presented a serious problem for drivers. For the first decade after they were introduced, cars with gasoline engines had to be started by turning a heavy iron crank located at the front of the vehicle.

Hand cranking an engine required considerable strength and was dangerous as well. Many men suffered broken arms from the back kick of the crank. Most women never even attempted to start an early gasoline-powered car.

In 1911, however, Charles F. Kettering introduced the electric starter. In 1912 he sold his invention to the Cadillac Motor Company, which immediately installed it in all of its cars. Soon, all gasoline-powered automobiles were equipped with the device. With the appearance of the self-starter, women returned to the driver's seat.

The Model T and its many imitators had made car ownership possible for almost all families. Automobile manufacturers, aware of the major role that wives played in a family's car-purchasing decision, began designing their automobiles with women in mind. Cars would become more softly sprung to cushion their ride. Steering mechanisms would be improved to make it easier for women to turn and park.

Fashions also changed. "The only thing about a car which a woman does not have to teach herself," stated *Outing* magazine in 1927, "is how to dress for it." Other magazines filled their pages with articles such as "What the Well Dressed Autoist Now Wears" and "How to Stay Stylish in an Open Car."

All types of clothing were designed to keep the female motorist fashionably up-to-date. Scarves and

Passengers wait patiently while a man attempts to start the car's engine by turning the heavy hand crank. Before the electric starter was available to the motoring public, getting the motor running was a true physical challenge.

veils held specially designed hats in place. "A visored cap is very smart headgear," observed the magazine *The Automobile,* "but be sure it precisely matches the coat." Women motorists, as well as many men, often adopted a long, neck-to-ankle coat. Designed to protect against the dust kicked up by the automobile, it was appropriately called a "duster." As more women became drivers, they changed more aspects of their appearance to make motoring more comfortable. For example, both skirts and hairstyles became shorter.

The extraordinary increase in the number of automobiles and drivers in the early years of the car led to the institution of both drivers' licenses and license plates. Drivers' licenses and the tests that led to their issuance were created to make certain that anyone driving a car knew how to control it and knew the rules of the road. License plates were created so that cars could be traced

Wearing a hat and long coat as protection from the dusty road, the woman on the cover of a 1906 calendar models what the well-dressed female driver was likely to wear.

24  Driving around the USA

The building of the nation's highway system prompted the publication of detailed road maps, many provided free at gas stations. The cover of this 1933 map produced by the Shell Oil Company displays colorful license plates issued by different states.

in case of theft and so that police and state motor vehicle officials could easily identify the owner of a particular car. In 1900, New York became the first state to require a driver to be licensed, and the first license was issued to a Mr. Harold Birnie. Over the years, drivers' licenses have become more than proof a person has passed certain requirements and has authority from the state to drive a motor vehicle. Now that a license features a photograph of the license holder, it has become the primary way people can prove theirs ages (in bars, for example) and identity (for boarding commercial airplanes, for instance).

License plates have had a much more colorful history. They actually date back to the Roman Empire, when each chariot owner was required to register his vehicle and place an identifying tag on it. In the earliest days of motoring in the United States, car owners were actually required to have a different plate on their vehicle for each state through which they passed. In 1903, Massachusetts became the first state to issue plates legal in every state. By 1918, every other state had followed suit, with Florida being the last. With their varying and often-changing colors, states' mottoes and the rarity of some of them, license plate collecting has become a major hobby in the United States. Today, thousands of people subscribe to license plate catalogs and related publications and attend regularly held license plate collectors' conventions throughout the nation.

The automobile offered Americans the greatest freedom of movement they had ever had. Car manufacturers, however, discovered that auto racing would accelerate automobile mania even further. Americans had long been fascinated with contests based on speed. Horse racing was the nation's most popular sport. For spectators, auto racing added a whole new dimension to their love of competition and speed. For car manufacturers, it provided the opportunity to display how fast and how far their cars could go.

The first organized automobile race in the United States was held on Thanksgiving day, 1895. A car built by the company owned by the Duryeas—the brothers

The Indianapolis Motor Speedway, which held its first races in 1909, has long been the site of the Indianapolis 500. Today the race attracts as many as 300,000 spectators while millions of others watch the event on television.

who had been the first to drive a gasoline-powered automobile in the United States—won the race. After that, hundreds of different auto races were staged, but the most popular by far was the Vanderbilt Cup Race.

William K. Vanderbilt, Jr., one of the wealthiest men in America, sponsored the race, held yearly on Long Island, New York. The first Vanderbilt Cup Race was held on October 4, 1904. More than 30,000 spectators showed up and lined the roads. They were completely unprepared for what they would encounter. Unaware of how fast the cars would approach them,

26   Driving around the USA

many onlookers pushed forward on the roadway and then had to dive into a ditch to avoid being hit by the speeding cars.

The next Vanderbilt Cup was held a year later and drew more than 350,000 spectators. This time some onlookers were actually injured when they were struck by speeding contestants. Still the race was so important to so many people that it was held for nine more years. By 1914, however, so many spectators lined the racecourse that only a narrow lane remained for the speeding cars. The crowds had become so large that the police could not control them and the Vanderbilt Cup was discontinued.

By this time, however, automobile racing had become an enormously popular spectator sport. Large, circular tracks from which onlookers could safely cheer on their favorites solved the problems encountered in the Vanderbilt Cup and other open road races. Tracks

This Haynes-Apperson advertisement targets women drivers by describing the car's simplicity and reliability.

Automania  27

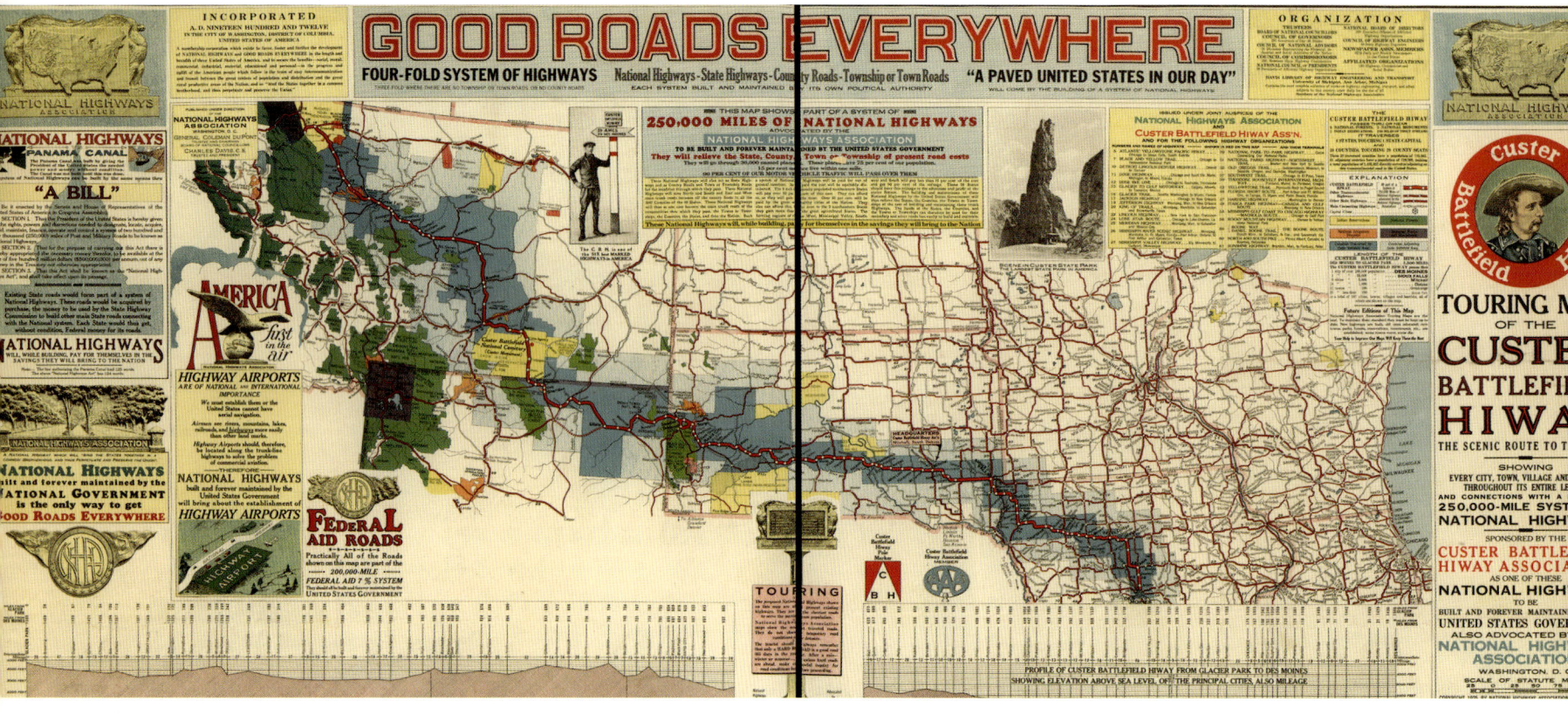

The ever-increasing popularity of the automobile led to the construction of highways and the improvement of existing roads. Historic sites such as the Custer Battlefield in Montana could advertise the fact that there were "good roads everywhere" that enabled visitors to reach them easily.

were built throughout the nation, but the most popular was the Indianapolis Speedway, which held its first race in 1911. Since then, the Indy 500, the speedway's annual 500-mile Memorial Day event, has remained the nation's most popular automobile race.

In the first quarter of the 1900s, long-distance automobile races were also staged to challenge the durability of both cars and drivers, rather than to test speed. The longest and perhaps strangest of these contests was an around-the-world race held in 1908. Six cars—three from France, one from Germany, one from Italy, and one from the United States—took part in the race, which was sponsored by two newspapers, the *New York Times* and *Le Matin* of Paris.

On February 12, 1908, some 50,000 people were on hand in Times Square in New York City as the competitors set off on their journey. The route of the race would take them across the United States to San Francisco, to Alaska by boat, on to Siberia, and then across Russia, Germany, Belgium, and France. Only three of the cars were able to complete the 13,341-mile race. The winner was a make of American car called a Thomas Flyer, which reached the finish line in Paris after 170 days.

Before average Americans could embark on long journeys, however, a nationwide system of roads and highways had to be built. Without such a system, the automobile would never have become the nation's favorite mode of transportation.

In 1904 there were only about 250 miles of paved or even loose-surfaced roads in the United States. As late as 1908, the year in which the Model T was launched, a writer for the magazine *Technical World* lamented that even in the populous state of New York, "no man can boast of traveling the entire 15 miles from Danville to Mount Morris in spring, for the road is impassable, as the broken-down wagons and buggies that line it from end to end bear mute witness."

Ironically, the motivation for building an adequate system of roads and highways in America came not from automobile interests but from those in support of another type of vehicle—the bicycle. In 1896, when fewer than 4,000 automobiles were registered in the United States, some 4 million bicycle riders were pedaling throughout the nation.

By the early 1900s, the number of bicyclists had grown to more than 10 million. Many of these bikers belonged to bicycle clubs such as the highly influential League of American Wheelmen. This organization persuaded the U.S. Congress to establish the Bureau of

Road Inquiry to investigate how to build an improved network of roads and highways.

As the automobile began to replace the bicycle, local automobile clubs around the nation began to take up the crusade to build better roads. The scattered local clubs lacked real power, but the better-roads movement took a positive turn in 1902 when the American Automobile Association (AAA) was formed. By 1910 the AAA had 25,000 members and had established strong affiliations with 225 local clubs throughout the United States. Groups that had a special interest in a highway system, including automobile manufacturers and oil company owners, joined the Automobile Association in lobbying Congress to build better roads.

In 1904, the pressure on Congress proved successful. The U.S. Office of Public Roads was formed. It began to distribute financial aid to various states to be used for building new roads and for surfacing existing ones. In 1916 Congress passed the Federal Aid Road Act, which allotted even larger sums to the states for the building and improvement of roads. Five years later, the Federal Highway Act was passed. It provided the funds for federal highways, integrated the nation's roads into federal and state systems, and created a unified system of numbering and marking the country's roads and highways. By the late 1920s, the United States had a system of paved arteries that could accommodate millions of motorists eager to travel.

In 1923, the American Automobile Association presented President Calvin Coolidge with his membership credentials. The first AAA club was formed in 1902 to improve road conditions.

Driving around the USA

# Route 66: The Mother Road

Of all the roads in the United States, the one with the most storied history is the highway called Route 66. The fabled road was commissioned in 1926, the year that the federal government began numbering U.S. highways. For most of the next quarter-century, it was the only major road to the West, stretching 2,448 miles, from Chicago to Santa Monica, California. In his novel *The Grapes of Wrath*, John Steinbeck wrote about how Route 66 was the artery over which tens of thousands of people traveled to California in the 1930s. They drove to escape the ravages of the Dust Bowl, a devastating drought that, in combination with increased farming, led to horrible dust storms and the destruction of many farms.

In the 1970s, nearly all of the original Route 66 was replaced by a modern four-lane highway. But it still winds its way through extraordinary scenery and still takes motorists past old diners, trading posts, historic motels, and other attractions. A true American phenomenon, Route 66 attracts people from all over the world who happily follow the path of what has affectionately become known as the "Mother Road."

This bumper sticker proudly proclaims that the driver has traveled along America's most famous highway.

CHAPTER 4

# The Indispensable Auto

*"The endless procession of automobiles fanning out into the country on a weekend [is evidence] of the hold the sport has taken on the popular fancy.... Sport? It is more than that, this automobilism; it is as necessary as the telephone and the typewriter."*

—*Independent Magazine,* 1923

In 1905 a prairie wife wrote to her sister in Boston and described the isolation she felt on her Nebraska farm: "I've lived through blizzards and drought,... I've seen our crops destroyed by hordes of grasshoppers. But what makes it all so hard is the loneliness. Our nearest neighbor is more than three miles away. The closest town is more than twenty miles further." For this woman and all those who lived in remote areas, the automobile would signal the end of isolation.

American doctors, like farmers, were among the first to take advantage of the automobile. The automobile made it easier for doctors to travel greater distances to reach a patient in need of medical attention. "The automobile," stated *Automobile* magazine in 1908,

has no more consistent and loyal set of users than the medical fraternity. First and foremost, the doctor insists on an automobile for business use; it will take him where he wants to go—where he is needed, often very urgently—in a fraction of the time any other method of transportation at his command could possibly do. It is scarcely to be wondered that doctors comprise a very large portion of the total of auto users.

Firemen in New York City pose atop their new engine around 1915. Motorized vehicles such as fire trucks, police cars, and ambulances made it possible for cities to serve and protect their citizens more effectively.

The automobile also changed the lives of people living on farms and in small towns by affecting rural education. Before the automobile, rural children attended small, local schools, most of which were under-equipped and too isolated to attract the best teachers. But with the school bus, rural communities could transport youngsters to a consolidated school and combine resources in order to better outfit it. Because teachers could get to these schools by automobile, more and better teachers accepted jobs, and the quality of teaching in rural America improved significantly.

The car also brought great changes to the city, not all of them positive. By the 1920s, automobiles clogged the streets. Combined with the trolleys that still moved along in great numbers over city streets, these vehicles created horrendous congestion. Today, most American cities are still struggling to resolve their traffic problems.

But city dwellers also greatly benefited from the automobile. Just as the car made it possible for rural folk to travel easily to the city, it enabled city inhabitants to escape the noise and congestion and to travel to places where the rail-bound trolleys and train could not go. "The endless procession of automobiles fanning out into the country on a weekend," observed *Independent Magazine* in 1923, "[is evidence] of the hold the sport has taken on the popular fancy. Sport? It is more than that, this automobilism; it is as necessary as the telephone and the typewriter."

Within the city, the introduction of the automobile improved municipal services. Although residents were fond of the horse-drawn firefighting brigades that raced through the streets, motorized fire engines were far faster and better equipped to put out fires.

Motorized vehicles with snowplows made snow removal, always a major problem in many cities, much more efficient. Motorized street sweepers kept city streets cleaner than before. And even though the police horse, like the fire horse, had long been regarded as a community pet, the police car almost immediately proved to be more effective in fighting crime. (As early automotive critics pointed out, however, the car also made it easier for criminals to flee.)

The automobile also accelerated the growth of the American suburbs. The trolley had made the suburb possible, but once commuters acquired cars, they no longer had to live near trolley or railroad lines.

In addition to changing Americans' personal lives, the automobile dramatically transformed the nation's economy. By the late 1920s—with more than 23 million cars on American roads and with about 85 percent of the world's motor vehicles being built in the United States—automaking became the nation's largest industry. Almost half a million men and women worked in automobile factories. And car manufacturers were the nation's largest customer as well. They annually purchased 90 percent of the nation's petroleum products, 80 percent of the rubber, 75 percent of the plate glass, 25 percent of the machine tools, and 20 percent of the steel. The industries that supplied such products employed more than 1.2 million people.

Auto-related businesses and accommodations, such as gas stations and repair shops, sprang up along the roadsides. In the early days of motoring, every driver had to be his own mechanic. As late as 1906, one of the most popular items in the

"The horsepower of an automobile may sometimes be judged by the number of horses required to haul it to the repair shop," read a joke from *Automobile Jokes, Jests, and Joshes*. But by the 1920s garages, such as this one in Wyoming's Yellowstone region, were able to keep most cars in good repair.

Hammacher Schlemmer Company's line of products was an 18-pound collection of tools that each motorist needed to fix his own car. By 1920, however, automobile repair shops were as common as hardware stores.

As more people traveled by car, the American landscape took on a whole new look. Roadside restaurants and food stands became popular. People who lived in small towns near major roads found that there was money to be made by renting out a spare bedroom or by building cabins on their property. The success of these small ventures led to more ambitious undertakings. Author Sinclair Lewis commented in the *Saturday Evening Post* in 1920:

> Somewhere in these states, there is a young man who is going to become rich. He is going to start a chain of small, clean pleasant hotels, standardized and nationally advertised, along every important motor route in the country. He is not going to waste money on gilt and onyx, but he is going to have agreeable clerks, good coffee, endurable mattresses and good lighting.

By the end of the 1920s, chains of motor hotels (the name was soon shortened to motels), very much like what Lewis described, were hosting millions of travelers.

Other touring motorists spent time at automobile camps that provided them with such comforts as hot and cold running water, showers, and laundry facilities. The first of these camps was built outside Denver in 1919. Within a decade, auto camping sites and trailer

The very first Holiday Inn, located in Memphis, Tennessee, attracted customers with its huge sign, which was visible from far down the road.

Driving around the USA

By making it easier for people to travel to and from the city, the automobile created an explosion in the growth of suburbs, communities that had first arisen with the coming of the trolley. This cluster of homes in Meridian, Idaho, is typical of many suburban areas.

The Indispensable Auto

parks were commonplace throughout the nation.

The motor hotels, the automobile camps, and the roadside restaurants were only the first types of businesses that made traveling by car more enjoyable and life in America more convenient. Soon there were drive-in banks and restaurants. By 1933 the first drive-in movie theaters had been introduced, enabling people to enjoy their favorite form of entertainment without having to leave their car.

Still, not everyone approved of the way the car was transforming the nation. Ministers complained that families

A capacity crowd enjoys a movie at a drive-in theater in Salt Lake City, Utah, in 1945. Drive-in-moviegoers enjoyed in-car speakers, in-car heaters, and refreshment stands.

were spending their Sundays on the highways rather than in church. Some people were upset that the automobile permitted young people to carry out their courting far away from parental supervision. And newspapers throughout the country voiced their alarm over the increasing number of deaths caused by automobile accidents.

Yet nothing could diminish Americans' love affair with the car. As millions of people took to the roads, often for the sheer pleasure of going someplace easily and inexpensively, the automobile became, as the *Boston Globe* put it, "the symbol of freedom, the badge of equality, and the vehicle of opportunity."

By the 1930s, Americans were not only in love with the automobile, but they would sacrifice almost anything rather than be without one. A nationwide survey concluded that "ownership of the automobile has now reached the point of being an essential part of normal living." Even in the worst days of the Great Depression in the late 1930s, five times as many American farmers owned automobiles as had running water.

To understand how indispensable the automobile had become, one had only to listen to the American public: "I'll go without food before I'll see us give up the car," exclaimed a Muncie, Indiana, woman in filling out a government survey. "I'd rather do without clothes than give up the car," stated a mother of nine. Yet another Muncie woman provided perhaps the most telling observation of all. When asked in the survey why her family maintained an automobile when it didn't even own a bathtub, she responded simply, "You can't go to town in a bathtub."

CHAPTER 5

# Classic Cars, Dream Machines, Hot Rods, and Lowriders

*"The Packard owner, however high his station, mentions his car with a certain satisfaction—knowing that his choice proclaims discriminating taste as well as a sound judgement of fine things."*

—Packard advertisement, 1937

Automobiles have come a long way since the days of the Model T, when most cars looked alike and were operated in the same way. The most visible change, particularly since the 1930s, has been in their styling. During the 1930s, a period regarded by car buffs as the automobile's golden age, automakers in the United States and around the world built what are now called classic cars.

The Lincoln Motor Company produced a typical line of such cars. Along with its standard models, Lincoln also provided customers with the option of ordering customized vehicles. Owners (for a price, of course) could specify the type of grillwork they wanted at the front of their car, what kind of seats they desired, and what features they wanted included on the dashboard. The Lincoln Continental, with its highly polished exterior, deep, rich upholstery, and long graceful lines, inspired New York's Metropolitan Museum of Art to cite it "for excellence as a work of art" in 1941.

Other examples of luxury cars were produced by the Pierce-Arrow Company. A favorite of American Presidents of the era, the Pierce-Arrow Runabout, which was first produced in 1927, was a two-seater that included an elegant toolbox and two rear-mounted spare tires. The company's Silver Arrow sedan, introduced in 1933, featured an all-steel top, 12-inch-thick doors, and spare wheels that were concealed within the car's front fenders. The car also featured a special type of rear window that, while giving its driver a clear view of the road behind, blocked the glare from the sun.

Throughout the 1930s, magazines in the United States and Europe were filled with beautiful advertisements aimed at those who could afford the luxury cars. Each carmaker took its own particular approach. The Packard Company, for example, emphasized the way its automobiles, unlike those of competing manufacturers, would remain "new" for years. Boasting that its styling was so superior that no yearly changes in design were necessary, Packard labeled

Automakers of the 1930s spared no expense in promoting their luxury cars. In order to capture the public's attention, many of their advertisements included illustrations by some of the nation's finest artists.

its product the "car of unchanging character." In Germany, Mercedes-Benz, which sold tens of thousands of vehicles in the United States, advertised itself as "the world's oldest and leading motor car makers." The company produced automobiles in which only the finest leather, wood, and metal were used. Its huge Model 540K was almost entirely handmade and is still regarded by many as the greatest luxury car of the era.

These cars and others made by companies such as Rolls-Royce in England were magnificent and lavish automobiles. They were also expensive. Prices for the luxury vehicles ranged from $5,000 to $15,000, as

Classic Cars, Dream Machines, Hot Rods, and Lowriders    41

compared to most cars which still sold for less than $1,000. But even in the hard economic times of the 1930s, makers of plush automobiles found enough customers to make these luxury models profitable.

But not all cars were built to attract purchasers looking for prestige. Automakers also designed machines aimed at attracting both the young and the young at heart. Two of the most popular, which also became classics, were the Stutz Bearcat and the Cord Roadster.

The Stutz Bearcat was first built about 1915 but was discontinued around 1920. Stutz revived the car in the early 1930s, adding a powerful eight-cylinder engine to the vehicle. (A cylinder is a chamber in which an automobile engine's piston moves compressed fuel and supplies power to the vehicle.) A beautifully appointed two-seater, the light but powerful Bearcat featured an indentation in the floorboard below the accelerator that allowed the operator to rest his heel while driving. The Cord Roadster, long and low-slung, was made distinctive by the hood, which ran a full half-length of its entire body.

As the final years of the 1930s approached, the public could only wonder what further automotive luxuries and exciting features lay ahead. But then, in 1939, Europe erupted into war. Two years later, the United States became embroiled in the conflict. Throughout the world, automakers ceased building cars for the public and turned their attention to making military vehicles and other armaments for the war effort.

When World War II ended in 1945, the American public was eager to see new cars. They were not disappointed. By 1950, millions of automobiles were once again rolling off the assembly lines. For the most part, they were very different from the cars that had been produced before the war. Automakers were keenly aware that most Americans, weary of the losses and hardships suffered during the conflict, were now seeking cars that were fun to drive and bolder in appearance than earlier models. Car buffs today refer to them as "dream machines."

With their extreme styling, many of these cars were among the longest and widest that had ever been built.

Some had panoramic windshields and kaleidoscopic color schemes. The most startling feature of all was the tail fin. Introduced by Cadillac in 1948, the tail fin set off a competition between automakers, who seemed to try to outdo each other by making the car with the longest fins. Some manufacturers produced models with fins so long that they stretched from the rear of the vehicle to the front door.

There were other radical features as well. Buicks had portholes in their fenders and distinctive grills that made it appear as if the cars were smiling. Some automobiles had bumpers that were shaped like rockets. Others had bullet-like taillights that stretched out from the fins. The Nash Rambler had front seats that could fold down into a bed. The rear seats in other cars could be folded down to carry cargo, the forerunner of today's hatchbacks. Hidden gas caps, buzzers that sounded when the driver exceeded the speed limit, bubble-top roofs, foot buttons to change radio stations, electric clocks—they were all part of what automotive buffs called cars with personality.

Tail fins are the most distinctive feature of many of the dream cars of the 1950s. These large, spectacular fins adorn a 1959 Cadillac Fleetwood.

During the 1950s and 1960s, the desire for cars that made a statement about the driver's identity also led to the appearance of two of the most customized types of automobiles ever created on a large scale. The first of these was the hot rod.

Many young men wanted to rebel against conformity and establish identities of their own. What better way than to take inexpensive cars called roadsters, strip them down, then soup them up and decorate them, in order to create a personalized vehicle far different from what their parents drove?

In the 1950s, in backyards, driveways, and high school shop classes throughout America, young people created hot rods by stripping their roadsters of fenders, bumpers, hoods, and windshields. They replaced the standard-sized tires with big ones in the back and small ones in the front. They painted bright flames or other designs on the bodies. And because speed and noise were signs of youthful rebellion, they adjusted the mufflers to produce a loud noise and modified the engines to make the cars go as fast as possible.

Young hot rod owners concentrated on not only the look and sound of their vehicles, they often also took on a whole new demeanor while driving them. "I owned a 1953 Mercury with three-inch lowering blocks, fender skirts, twin aerials, and custom upholstering made of rolled Naugahyde," American author Harry Crews commented in *Motor Age* magazine in 1992.

> Staring into the bathroom mirror for long periods of time I practiced expressions to drive it with. It was that kind of car. It looked mean, and it was mean. Consequently it had to be handled with a certain style. One-handing it through a ninety-degree turn on city streets in a power slide…you were obligated to have your left arm hanging half out the window and a very bored expression on your face.…

Hot-rodders congregated at drive-in restaurants and drive-in theaters, where they showed off their creations. They also captured attention by proudly driving the noisy vehicles through city streets. And they held impromptu hot-rod races wherever they could find large open areas. Today hot rods are prized not as

John F. Kennedy waves to admirers during his 1960 presidential campaign. American Presidents have long used the automobile both on campaign tours and on official business.

Classic Cars, Dream Machines, Hot Rods, and Lowriders     45 vehicles to be driven, but as motorized artistic treasures passed on from generation to generation, and they are often on display at custom car rallies.

Hot rods were not the only automobiles created for a special social purpose. Just as the hot rods grew out of the youth rebellion of the 1950s, a car known as the lowrider emerged as a symbol used by Mexican Americans to call attention to themselves to protest ethnic discrimination. Mexican Americans customized slow-moving vehicles of many different makes to ride close to the ground. Unlike hot rods, these cars were to be judged not on their speed but on the beauty of their painted decorations and adornments.

Using the cars to proclaim their identity, Mexican Americans continue to paint murals on them that depict aspects of their culture and religion, as well as fantasy. They also give the cars multicolored paint jobs and often equip them with small gold-plated wire wheels

This issue of *Honk!* magazine from 1953 offered dedicated hot rodders tips on how to care for and customize their cars.

Driving around the USA

The owner of this lowrider personalized his car by painting a mural on its trunk and roof. Lowriders are a unique product of the Mexican and California car culture.

and trims. Because, for added effect, lowriders are slung so low, often violating automotive safety codes, many owners have installed hydraulic systems that allow them to instantly raise the cars to legal heights whenever a police officer comes into view.

Today, lowriders remain a means of Mexican-American self-expression and identity. Like the hot rods before them, they provide their owners with pride of craftsmanship, a sense of community, and a way to acknowledge their heritage.

Classic Cars, Dream Machines, Hot Rods, and Lowriders

# CHAPTER 6
# The Car Culture

*"It is probable that no invention…so quickly exerted influences that ramified through the national culture, transforming even habits of thought and language."*

—Presidential committee report on the impact of the automobile, 1934

Today, more than 133 million cars are registered in the United States. In a nation where it is as common for women as well as men to be employed, often at a considerable distance from home, families often own two cars. For many, carpooling has replaced the school bus as a means of transporting children to and from school.

Cars have evolved over the years to reflect changing American lifestyles. As outdoor recreational pursuits have become increasingly popular, many families have purchased spacious sport-utility vehicles (SUVs), vans, and station wagons. And as American families' incomes have increased and their vacations become considerably longer and more frequent, larger vehicles allow families to travel with whatever gear they need. In a nation where organized sports for both boys and girls have grown dramatically in recent years, "soccer moms" and other parents have addressed the problem of transporting their children, their friends, and their gear to games and practices by purchasing these multi-seated vehicles.

Pickup trucks, once used almost exclusively by farmers, builders, and repairmen, have also become popular, particularly as second cars. Today's pickup

During the gasoline crisis of the 1970s, gas station owners were forced to limit the number of gallons of gas customers could purchase.

trucks have many of the amenities (air-conditioning, power steering, and CD players, for example) of the finest automobiles.

The car changed not only how Americans traveled but also how goods were transported. Soon after the car was developed, the earliest trucks appeared, in the mid-1890s. Originally called power wagons, they ran on steam or electricity, had solid rubber tires and crude springs, and gave both driver and cargo an extremely rough ride. Still, they were more efficient for transporting freight than the horse-drawn wagons they would ultimately replace. As one early truck advertisement proclaimed, "The power wagon will do the work of three or more horse-drawn wagons—and do it better and cheaper."

By 1918 there were more than 600,000 trucks in operation in the United States. By 1940 more than half of the communities in America received their goods exclusively by truck. Today, trucks of every size and

The Car Culture

Trucks, ranging in size from large lumber-hauling vehicles and double-length tractor trailers to small pickups, carry all types of goods, from lumber to livestock.

variety—ranging from small vans to huge dump trucks and cement mixers to triple trailers—have become more important and more commonplace than ever. Some 9 million of these vehicles are in service on our nation's roads. They play a vital role in the construction business and haul more than 75 percent of the country's industrial products. Trucks transport almost everything we eat, wear, and use at some point in a product's journey from factory to store.

"There's a lot of tough things about this job," says long-distance truck driver Frank Salata, Jr.,

> I'm on the road for hours at a stretch and there's all kinds of weather to contend with. I'm given a tight schedule but road construction that I run into everywhere and accidents caused by crazy drivers make that a real challenge. Still, the pay is really good, and I love being on the road. And even though I know it sounds corny, I really believe I'm doing something important. A lot of what we truck drivers deliver keeps this country going.

At the other end of the automotive spectrum are the compact cars. During the 1960s, foreign carmakers, particularly those in Japan and Germany, began exporting automobiles to the United States in great numbers. By 1965, Americans were buying more than 400,000 foreign-made cars every year. Many of these cars were much smaller and more economical to purchase and maintain than American models. They were also more fuel efficient—traveling more miles for every gallon of gasoline—than the larger, heavier cars made in the United States. In the late 1970s, when gasoline supplies became limited and gas prices rose dramatically, the smaller foreign cars became increasingly popular with American buyers. In response, U.S. companies began

Following the passage of the National Highway Act in 1956, the construction of wide-laned expressways and interchanges, such as this one in Los Angeles, changed the American landscape.

The Car Culture

turning out their own compact cars. Today, with gasoline prices still fluctuating, every major American car manufacturer includes at least one compact or even subcompact model in its product line.

Among the most notable of these compact cars is the Volkswagen Beetle, first produced in Germany by the Porsche Motor Company and first introduced into the United States in 1949. Inexpensive (a new Beetle costs about $1,600), extremely fuel efficient and easy to maintain, the small, uniquely shaped vehicle caught on immediately with American car buyers. Between 1949 and 1977 more than 21 million Beetles were sold in the United States. "The Beetle," wrote former Volkswagen advertising executive John Slavin, in *Advertising Age* magazine in 1998, "had a unique, magnificent history of being a trusted friend." He might have added that no other automobile in history has been the star of four Walt Disney movies: *The Love Bug, Herbie Rides Again, Herbie Goes To Monte Carlo,* and *Herbie Goes Bananas.*

By 1978 many other types of compact cars had been introduced, and Beetle sales declined to a point where Volkswagen halted production. In 1998, however, Volkswagen introduced a brand new Beetle, complete with front-wheel drive and other mechanical improvements. But it is the Beetle of the 1950s, 60s, and 70s that retains its cult status, an automobile that, in the words of John Slavin, "…became the stereotypical symbol of happy, fun-loving people."

One of the most significant developments in modern automotive history has been the growth of the car rental business. Today, millions of Americans use rental cars for either business or pleasure every year. The rental car business had its beginnings only a few years after Henry Ford introduced the Model T. A Nebraskan named Joe Saunders is credited with having started the first such enterprise when in 1916, he began loaning out his Model T to traveling salesmen. The first major rental-car company was established in 1918 when John Hertz formed what became known as Hertz Drive-Ur-Self System.

Herbie the Love Bug stars in four Walt Disney movies as a mystery-solving Volkswagen Beetle that can fly.

Driving around the USA

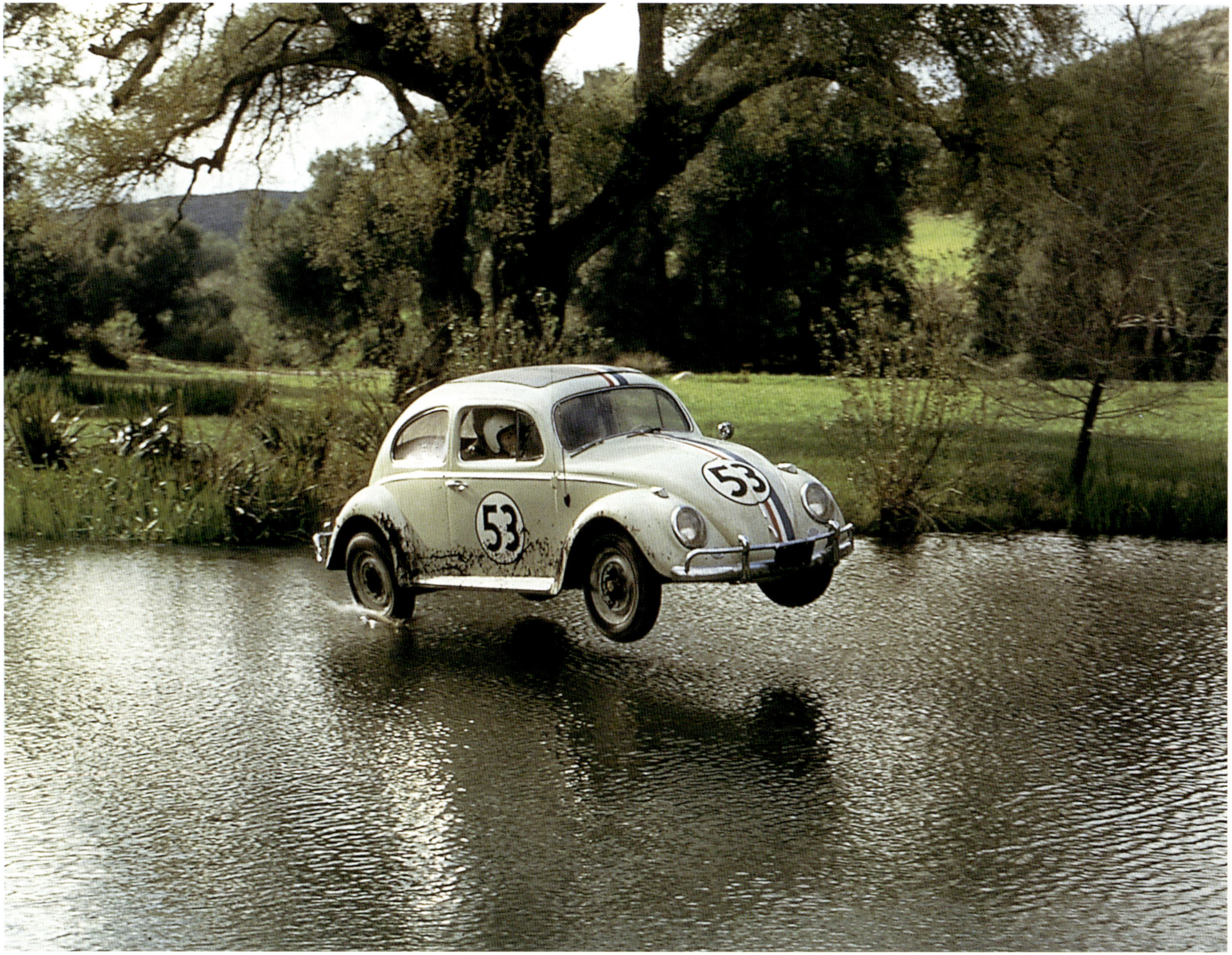
53
53

Hertz's business prospered, and soon several competitors formed their own companies. In an interesting development, many of the cars loaned out by these early companies were rented by people involved in crime. The 1920s was a time of widespread gangster activity, and criminals, renting cars under assumed names, often used the vehicles to carry out bank robberies and other illegal activities.

In the 1930s, however, car rental regained respectability and business boomed. Much of the growth was connected with the railroads. As increasing numbers of travelers, particularly businessmen, used the train, they discovered that renting a car to travel to and from the railroad terminals was often more convenient than using their own automobiles. In response, the rental car companies began setting up rental booths within the stations.

The rental car industry grew even more rapidly during the 1950s with the boom in the airline industry. As people traveled longer distances for greater periods of time, many found that renting a car to journey to and from the airport was preferable to paying the large parking fees charged at airport garages. For businessmen traveling to distant cities, rental cars that would allow them to visit their customers miles away from the airport became (and remains) an absolute necessity.

The presence of so many automobiles on American streets and highways in modern times has caused many problems, not the least of which is an extravagant use of energy and the release of pollutants into the environment. This has been particularly true of one of the most popular of today's vehicles, the SUV. In 1985, SUVs accounted for only 2 percent of new vehicle sales. Today, one out of every four vehicles purchased in the United States is an SUV, and sales continue to climb.

In their television, radio, and print advertisements the automobile industry portrays SUVs as the ticket to the outdoors. Commercials depict them carrying happy drivers and passengers up steep, snow-capped mountains, across desert sand dunes, and through the wilderness. In reality, only about 5 percent of SUVs are ever taken off-road. The great majority are used for everyday driving.

A driver's education instructor prepares his student to take the road test necessary to earn a driver's license. Driver's ed courses, conducted both in public high schools and by private companies, have resulted in better drivers and improved highway safety.

According to the U.S. Environmental Protection Agency (EPA), driving fuel-efficient vehicles is one of the most important things that Americans can do to reduce global warming, which is the increase in the temperature of the earth's atmosphere caused by pollutants. According to the Sierra Club, if you drove a 13-mile-per-gallon SUV (rather than an average 22-mile-per-gallon car) for just one year, you would waste more energy than if you left your refrigerator door open for 6 years or left your color television set turned on for 28 years or left your bathroom light on for 30 years.

Thanks to strict anti-pollution regulations that the federal government has imposed on carmakers, automotive pollution has been dramatically reduced. In the last three decades, for example, the use of catalytic converters (devices on automobiles that convert carbon monoxide and other pollutants into carbon dioxide and water) has played an important role in this reduction. So, too, has the nationwide switch from pollution-causing leaded fuel to far cleaner unleaded gasoline. Together these two developments have reduced tailpipe pollution by more than 97 percent.

The Car Culture

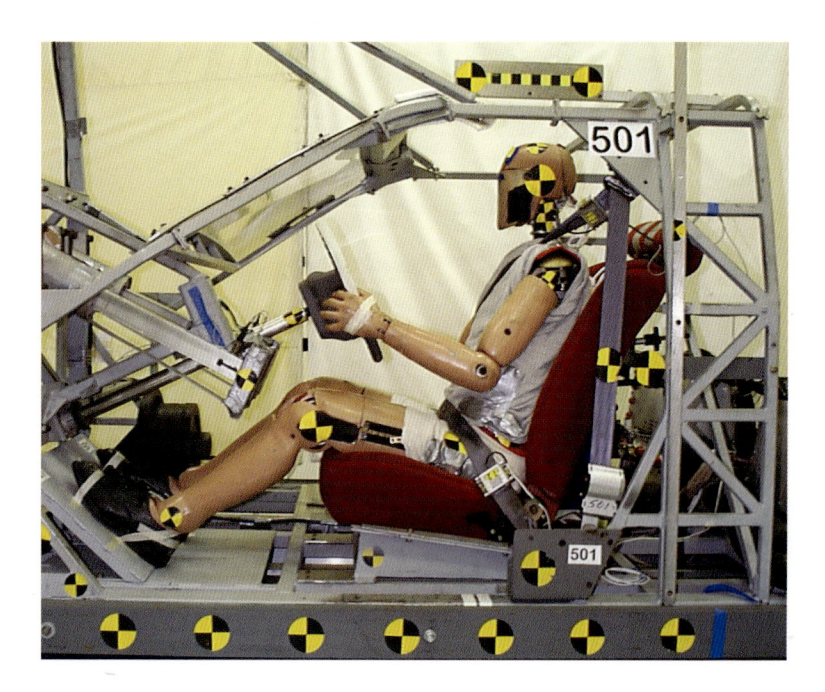

This crash-test dummy named THOR registers 250 measurements 10,000 times every second during a simulated crash. This information is used to design cars that are better able to protect their occupants.

The cars of the future will, most likely, be even less polluting and more fuel-efficient. Toyota and Honda, for example, now offer cars that, in addition to using gasoline, can also be powered by electric batteries. Other car companies may well follow suit.

The most serious of all the problems connected with the enormous amount of automobile traffic in the United States is that of automobile accidents. In 1998, more than 41,000 Americans were killed in automobile-related accidents, and more than 3 million others were injured.

In the last 20 years, both the national government and state agencies have taken significant steps to make travel by automobile safer. In the 1990s, new laws required automakers to install air bags in their vehicles. And in the late 1990s, many states made the use of seat belts mandatory, and imposed strict fines on both drivers and passengers caught failing to do so.

Many states, with the aid of federal funding, have also undertaken construction programs designed to straighten out dangerous curves in their roads and to remove other highway hazards. Various states have also replaced antiquated traffic lights with signals that are easier to see and timed specifically to traffic patterns. School-sponsored driver education programs and mandatory use of children's car seats have also improved traffic safety.

Computers will play an ever-increasing role in the automotive world. Cars are now designed, engineered, and assembled with the constant aid of computers. Car inspection, servicing, and repair have also been computerized. And drivers rely on computers to make their ride easier, safer, and more comfortable. Some automobiles, for example, have computerized suspension systems that allow the car to adjust to changes in the road surface. Other cars warn drivers when they come too close to other vehicles while parking. Thanks to the computer, many of today's automobiles are even equipped with special systems that give the driver precise directions to a destination. Such systems also indicate the number of miles to that spot, the amount of fuel that will be consumed, and the estimated time of arrival, based on how fast the vehicle travels.

While technical changes continue to take place, so too will changes on the business side of manufacturing cars. Automakers have been forced to produce an increasing range of models to satisfy public demand. In 1999, for instance, two of the world's largest car makers, BMW and Audi, each had 59 different versions of their cars on the market. The demands made on automakers and the increasing cost of producing cars has put a number of major automakers in financial trouble, forcing some to sell out to other manufacturers. Between 1998 and 2000, the Ford Motor Company purchased Volvo, Chrysler purchased Daimler-Benz, and Volkswagen bought Bentley, Bugatti, Lamborghini, and Rolls-Royce.

In the early 1930s, President Herbert Hoover established a committee to study what factors had most influenced American life to that time. In its final report to the President, the committee stated that it was the automobile that had brought about the most meaningful and far-reaching changes: "It is probable that no invention…so quickly exerted influences that ramified

An SUV makes its way over terrain that a standard automobile would find difficult, if not impossible, to maneuver. Responding to both public and government pressure, SUV makers have pledged to make their vehicles more fuel efficient.

through the national culture, transforming even habits of thought and language."

The committee was right. And, if anything, the automobile has had an even greater impact on American life in the decades following the committee report. Wayne Paddock, the owner of several optometry stores on Cape Cod, Massachusetts, owns five cars, ranging form a vintage Ford Mustang convertible to a luxurious Lincoln Town Car. He is also the president of his local automobile club. Paddock speaks for the legions of car enthusiasts around the nation when he describes what, to him, are the greatest attributes of the automobile. "My cars allow me to go fast, which I love; they allow me to tinker with them mechanically, which I also like. But it's the freedom to go anywhere, any time I want that I think is the automobile's greatest gift."

58   Driving around the USA

# Timeline

**1769**
Nicolas Joseph Cugnot builds and drives the first self-propelled road vehicle

**1891**
William Morrison builds America's first successful electric car

**1893**
Charles and Frank Duryea drive a gasoline-powered car through the streets of Springfield, Massachusetts

**1896**
F. E. and F. O. Stanley begin building steam-driven cars in Newton, Massachusetts

**1900**
First automobile advertisement appears in the *Saturday Evening Post*; New York issues first driver's license

**1901**
Ransom E. Olds introduces mass-production techniques to the automobile industry

**1902**
American Automobile Association established

**1908**
First Model T Ford produced; New York–to–Paris road race is won by a Thomas Flyer automobile

**1911**
Charles Kettering invents the electric starter; first Indianapolis 500 auto race is held.

**1913**
Ford produces 1,000 cars in one day

**1923**
Hertz becomes first national car-rental agency

**1933**
Nation's first drive-in movie theater opens in New Jersey

**1942**
Civilian production of automobiles is halted for World War II

**1945**
Civilian production of automobiles resumes

**1948**
Jeep wagon (arguably the first sport-utility vehicle) introduced

**1949**
Volkswagen Beetle introduced to the United States

**1955**
Nine million cars are produced in the United States, a new production record

**1984**
First minivans produced by American car makers

**1993**
SUVs capture a major share of the American auto market

**1995**
Global Positioning System is introduced in American automobiles

**1999**
First production-level gasoline-electric hybrid

**2002**
First consumer fuel cell vehicle sold in the United States

# Places to Visit

Below is a list of museums that display automobiles from every era and objects related to the automotive history. Most of these museums also feature films and photographic exhibits depicting the role of the automobile in American life. Many also offer rides in early and classic cars.

### California

NHRA Motorsports Museum
Fairplex Gate 1
1101 West McKinley Avenue
Pomona, CA
909-622-2133
www.nhra.com/musuem

Towe Auto Museum
2200 Front Street
Sacramento, CA 95818
916-442-6802
www.toweautomuseum.org

### Florida

Fort Lauderdale Antique Car Museum
1527 Packard Avenue
Fort Lauderdale, FL 33315
954-779-7300
www.antiquecarmuseum.org

### Kentucky

Swope's Cars of Yesterday Museum
1100 North Dixie Avenue
Elizabethtown, KY 42701
270-765-2181
www.swopemusuem.com

### Massachusetts

Larz Anderson Auto Museum
Larz Anderson Park
15 Newton Street
Brookline, MA 02455
617-522-6547
www.mot.org

### Michigan

Henry Ford Museum & Greenfield Village
20900 Oakwood Boulevard
Dearborn, MI 48124
313-982-6100
www.hfmgv.org

### Nevada

National Automobile Museum
Mill Street at Lake Street
Reno, NV 89501
775-333-9300
www.automuseum.org

### New York

The Museum of Automobile History
321 North Clinton Street
Syracuse, NY 13202
315-478-2277
www.themuseumofautomobilehistory.com

### Ohio

Canton Classic Car Museum
Market Avenue at Sixth Street
Canton, OH 44702
330-455-3603
www.cantonclassiccar.org

### Pennsylvania

Swigart Museum
Route 22, 3 1/2 miles east of Huntingdon
Huntingdon, PA 16652
814-643-0885
www.swigartmuseum.com

# Further Reading

Adler, Dennis. *The Art of the Automobile: The 100 Greatest Cars.* New York: HarperCollins, 2000.

Batchelor, Dean. *The American Hot Rod.* Osceola, Wisc.: Motorbooks Publishing, 1995.

Bourne, Russell. *Americans on The Move.* Golden, Colo.: Fulcrum, 1995.

Boyne, Walter. *Power Behind the Wheel: Creativity and Evolution of the Automobile.* New York: Stewart, Tabori & Chang, 1988.

Burness, Tad. *Ultimate Auto Album: An Illustrated History of the Automobile.* New York: Krause, 2002.

Coffey, Frank, et al. *America on Wheels: The First Hundred Years.* New York: General Publishing Group, 1996.

Donnelly, Nora, ed. *Customized: Art Inspired by Hot Rods, Low Riders, and American Car Culture.* New York: Abrams, 2000.

Falk, Duane. *Legends of the Track: Great Moments in Stock Car Racing.* New York: Metro, 2001.

Finch, Christopher. *Highways to Heaven: The Auto Biography of America.* New York: HarperCollins, 1992.

Flower, Raymond, and Michael Jones. *100 Years on The Road, A Social History of the Car.* New York: McGraw-Hill, 1981.

Georgano, Nick, Bengt Holm, and Michael Sedgwick. *Cars, 1930–2000: The Birth of the Modern Car.* New York: Todtri Productions, 2001.

Hirsch, Jay. *Great American Dream Machines: Classic Cars of the 50s and 60s.* New York: Macmillan, 1985.

McNalley, Bruce. *Model T Ford: The Car that Changed the World.* Osceola, Wisc.: Motorbooks Publishing, 1994.

Miller, Denis. *The Illustrated History of Trucks and Buses.* London: Quarto, 1982.

Sandler, Martin W. *This Was America.* Boston: Little, Brown, 1980.

Witzul, Michael. *Route 66 Remembered.* Osceola, Wisc.: Motorbooks Publishing, 1996.

# Index

References to illustrations are indicated by page numbers in **bold**.

## A
Accidents, 39, 56–57
Advertising, **19**, **25**–**27**, 40, **41**, 49, 52, 54, 59
American Automobile Association (AAA), **30**, 59
Automobile camps, 36–38
Automobile clubs, 30, 58

## B
Beetle. *See* Volkswagen Beetle
Benz, Karl, 12
Birth of automobiles, 7–9
Buick (car), 43
Buick automobile factory, **18**

## C
Car buffs, 42–43, 58
Car culture, 48–58
City life and cars, 11, 15, 32, 34
Classic cars, 40–42, 60
Compact cars, 51–52
Cord Roadster (car), 42
Crank starter, 22–**23**
Crash-test dummy, **56**
Cugnot, Nicolas Joseph, 7–9, 59
Culture of the car, 48–58
Custer Battlefield Hiway, **28**
Customized cars, 40, 44–47, 60

## D
Daimler, Gottlieb, 12
Deaths in car accidents, 39, 56
*Detroit Industry* (mural, Diego Rivera), **20**
Dream machines, 42–**43**
Drive-in businesses, **38**, 44, 59
Driver education programs, **55**, 57
Drivers' licenses, 24–25
Duryea, Charles and Frank, 12, 14–15, 26, 59

## E
Early cars, 14–21
Electric cars, 11–12, 15–16, 56, 59
Electric starter, 23
Energy problems, 54
European experiments, 7–9, 12
Evans, Oliver, 8

## F
Family life and cars, 38–39, 48
Farming life and cars, 32, 34, 39
Fashion and cars, 23–**24**
Fire trucks, **33**–34
Ford, Henry, **15**, 18–19, 21
Foreign-made import cars, 51–52
Freedom of movement, 6–7, **17**, 26, 32, 34, 39, 58
Fuel cell vehicles, 56, 59
Fuel efficiency, 11, 51–52, 55–56

## G
Gas crisis, **49**, 51
Gas stations, **25**, 35
Gasoline, 49, **51**, 55. *See also* Fuel efficiency
Gasoline engine, 12, 22–23, 42, 55
Gas-powered cars, **10**, 12, 14–23, 26
General Motors Company, 22
Global Positioning System (GPS), 59

## H
Hatchbacks, 43
Haynes-Apperson (car), **27**
Herbie the Love Bug (Volkswagen Beetle, movie star), 52–**53**
Hertz, John, 52, 54
Hertz Drive-Ur-Self System, 52, 54, 59
Highway construction, **25**, 28–31, **51**. *See also* Roads, road improvements
Holiday Inn (motel), **36**
Hoover, Herbert, 57
Hot rods, 44, 46
Hybrid fuel-electric cars, 56, 59

## I
Indianapolis 500, Indianapolis Speedway, **26**, 28, 59
Indispensability, 32–39
Internal combustion engine. *See* Gasoline engine

## J
Jeep wagon (car), 59

62 Index

## K
Kettering, Charles F., 23, 59

## L
Leaded gasoline, 55
License plates, 24–**25**
Lifestyles and cars, 40, 48, 57–58
Lincoln Town Car, 58
Love affair with the car, 39
Lowriders, 46–**47**
Luxury cars, 22, 40–42, 58

## M
Mass production, manufacturing, 15–16, 18, **18**, 21, 59
Mechanics, **16**, 21, 35
Mexican Americans. *See* Lowriders
Mileage. *See* Fuel efficiency
Minivans, 59
Model 540K Mercedes-Benz (car), 41
Model R, Model S Ford (car), 22
Model T Ford (car), **15**, 19, 21, 23, 29, 52, 59
Morrison, William, 11, 59
Motor hotels (motels), 36, 38
Municipal services and motorized vehicles, 34
Museums, 60
Mustang (car), 58

## N
Nash Rambler (car), 43
Numbers of cars, 21–22, 35, 48–49, 54, 58–59

## O
Olds, Ransom E., 14, 16, 18, 21, 59
Olds Motor Works (Oldsmobile Company), 16, 18–**19**

## P
Packard (car), 40, **41**
Pickup trucks, 48–50
Pierce-Arrow Runabout (car), 40–41
Pierce-Arrow Silver Arrow (car), 41
Police cars, 33–34
Pollution problems, 54–56
Prices, 16, 18, 21, 41–42, 52

## R
Races, racing, **26**–29, 44
Rental car businesses, 52, 54, 59
Repair shops, **35**–36
River Rouge Factory (Ford), **20**, 21
Road maps, **25**, **28**
Roads, road improvements, 22, **28**–30, 56–57. *See also* Highway construction
Roadside businesses, services, 35–36, 38
Route 66, the "Mother Road," 31
Rural life and cars, 32, 34

## S
Safety improvements, 56–57
School buses, 34
Selden, George B., 12
Songs, **16**
Sport-utility vehicles (SUVs), 48, 54–55, **58**–59
Stanley, Francis E. and Freelan O., 9–10, 59

Stanley Steamer, **9**–10
Station wagons, 48
Steam tricycle, 7
Steam-driven vehicles (steamers), 7–12
Stutz Bearcat (car), 42
Styling, 40, 42–43
Subcompact cars, 52
Suburban life and cars, 35, **37**
Symbolism of cars, 39

## T
Tail fins, **43**
Thomas Flyer (car), 29, 59
Tin Lizzie. *See* Model T Ford (car)
Traffic accidents. *See* Accidents
Traffic problems, 34
Trailer parks, 36–37
Trevithick, Richard, 8–9
Trucks, 48–51

## U
Unleaded gasoline, 55

## V
Vanderbilt, William K., Jr., 26
Vanderbilt Cup Race, 26–27
Vans, 48, 50, 59
Volkswagen Beetle, **49**, 52–**53**, 59

## W
Women and cars, 11, 22–24, **27**, **41**
World War II and cars, 42, 59

**Martin W. Sandler** is the author of more than 40 books. His *Story of American Photography: An Illustrated History for Young People* received the Horn Book Award in 1984. Sandler's other books include *America, A Celebration!, Photography: An Illustrated History, The Vaqueros: The World's First Cowmen,* and the Library of Congress American history series for young adults. An accomplished television producer and writer as well, Sandler has received Emmy and Golden Cine awards for his television series and programs on history, photography, and American business. He has taught American studies to students in junior high and high school, as well as at the University of Massachusetts and Smith College. He lives in Cotuit, Massachusetts, with his wife, Carol.

### Other titles in the Transportation in America series include:

*Galloping across the USA: Horses in American Life*

*On the Waters of the USA: Ships and Boats in American Life*

*Riding the Rails in the USA: Trains in American Life*

*Straphanging in the USA: Trolleys and Subways in American Life*

*Flying over the USA: Airplanes in American Life*